The Other Side
of the Coyne

The Other Side
of the Coyne

Douglas Wilson

canonpress
Moscow, Idaho

Table of
Contents

Mobius Strip Reason

I t has been a while since I have gone through a book chapter by chapter and, weather permitting, the next one I shall attempt is *Why Evolution is True* by Jerry Coyne.[1] Coyne is a big-time Johnny in the world of evolution, so I will definitely be punching up out of my weight class. The closest I have ever gotten to the big-time in the world of evolution was that tour of the Smithsonian I took as a kid.

This review of his preface will serve, in a neat, chiastic way, as my preface to the review. Coyne begins by discussing a legal fracas in 2005 in Dover, Pennsylvania, a case precipitated by a school board instructing that the ninth graders under their charge be told that evolution was a theory, not a fact, that they ought to keep an open mind, and that the book *Of Pandas and People* was available to them in case they wanted to check it out for themselves. Of course, planes started falling from the sky at the very prospect, and the trial would have gone very badly for the Truth had not Bruce

---

1. Jerry Coyne, *Why Evolution is True* (Oxford University Press, 2009).

Willis parachuted in and saved the judge from those hostage-taking creationists who had him in a back room and were showing him flannelgraph pictures of Noah's Ark. Still, for all that, it was a close call.

In his preface, Coyne complains about the staying power of creationism. He says that (in the trial) "*Of Pandas and People* was shown to be a put-up job, a creationist book in which the words 'creation' had simply been replaced by the words 'intelligent design'" (p. xii). He says a moment later that the judge, deciding for evolution, had opined that "intelligent design was just recycled creationism" (p. xii). And he gives us credit for being . . . um . . . pretty resilient. "Creationism is like the inflatable roly-poly clown I played with as a child: when you punch it, it briefly goes down, but then pops back up" (p. xiii). And as if I were trying to make this particular point for him, here I show up reviewing his book, with a red nose and as irrational as all get-out.

But let me begin my engagement with Coyne with a brief, flickering moment of agreement. One evolutionary scientist once said that intelligent design was simply creationism in a cheap tuxedo. I agree with the central point there, but I actually think it is a very fine tuxedo. Many of the ID folks simply want to maintain that the world around us exhibits design, meaning there was a *some* kind of designer, and they are not saying who that designer might be. Might be God, who knows, might be somebody else. Right. We are not saying that it was God who created the world . . . just someone with the same skill set.

This ID coyness really has been unfortunate. If the designer of this world who scattered evidences of design throughout His handiwork is God, well, then, there you are—creationism. But if that designer is not God, but rather a really smart angel/alien, what ID argument from design could not be applied to *him*? Does not this non-Deity creator of the whole shooting match exhibit at least as much design as, say, mitochondria? A 3-D printer that prints, say, a domino, has printed a domino that exhibits design. But when my gaze moves from the domino to the printer itself, why do I have to stop asking questions? That exhibits a heckuva lot *more* design, if you ask me, which you should.

But my agreement with Coyne on this point really is fleeting. The arguments of ID, although unfortunately mislocated by many ID advocates on the cosmic flow chart, are nonetheless unanswerable by someone in Coyne's position. It is high dogma with these guys that materialism is an axiomatic given. In their minds, no scientific evidence, by definition, can legitimately lead to a questioning of this materialism. This is his *faith* position, and let us be blunt—this was not something that was scientifically ascertained. What scientific experiment could possibly be constructed, or scientific computer model programmed, that would show that the only way to find out anything whatever is through such experiments and modeling? This is not reason—it is Mobius strip reason. What my net don't catch ain't fish.

Coyne is unable to answer the ID challenge on two levels. The first is within the framework of science and reason that he accepts as given, a framework that collides with his *a priori* materialism. With regard to the first framework, if confronted with an argument from (say) irreducible complexity, he has to say (instead of answering the argument) that only a creationist would argue from irreducible complexity. Okay, and at least I grant the point. Now, how about it? Tell me how a small wooden platform can catch mice in the course of its evolution up to a working mechanism that catches mice more efficiently.

The second framework is his materialism, which renders all argumentation—whether in favor of evolution or not—absurd. Coyne revealed his hard materialism when he wrote elsewhere that "the view that all sciences are *in principle* reducible to the laws of physics must be true unless you're religious." But if our thoughts are simply what these chemicals in my bone box do under these conditions and at this temperature, then (of course) I have no reason for supposing my beliefs to be true. But—and follow me closely here—this would include the belief that my bone box has any chemicals in it, or that my chemicals have a bone box to hold them. The belief that the universe is simply and solely atoms in motion has a hard time accounting for the existence of anything that would not be atoms in motion. But my knowledge that the universe is atoms in motion is not . . . wait for it . . . is not atoms in motion. Knowledge is as immaterial as the Queen of Fairie. Farley's ghost, call your office.

Coyne wants this volume of his to give "a succinct summary of why modern science recognizes evolution as true" (p. xiv). And in the spirit of good sportsmanship, I would like to wish him luck.

CHAPTER 1

Occam's Shaving Kit

Jerry Coyne's first chapter of *Why Evolution Is True* begins with something of a patronizing quotation from Jacques Monod: "A curious aspect of the theory of evolution is that everybody thinks he understands it" (p. 1) Well, excuse us.

But after that, he starts at the right place, which is the appearance of design. Coyne quotes Paley's form of the argument from design,[2] which he then calls "both commonsensical and ancient" (p. 2). Beginning this way, Coyne acknowledges that evolutionists must walk up something of an incline until we all come out on the sunny uplands of enlightenment. That incline is the fact that the *appearance* of design is all around us. Coyne believes, however, that if we just define our terms properly, the problem evaporates.

Let me begin with his definition on evolution, followed by a brief definition of the six constituent elements of it.

---

2. William Paley's *Natural Theology* proposed the now famous "watchmaker" analogy (the existence of a watch implies the existence of a watchmaker).

"Life on earth evolved gradually beginning with one primitive species—perhaps a self-replicating molecule—that lived more than 3.5 billion years ago; it then branched out over time, throwing off many new and diverse species; and the mechanism for most (but not all) of evolutionary change is natural selection" (p. 3).

The six components of this are as follows—evolution, gradualism, speciation, common ancestry, natural selection, and evolutionary change by nonselective means (p. 3). Evolution means that genetic changes occur over time. Gradualism means that the time involved is a long time. Speciation means that different groups split, and go their separate ways, developing in different directions over time. Common ancestry is the "flip side of speciation" (p. 8), pointing out that all these variegated species didn't used to be variegated—they came from a common source. Natural selection is what accounts for the appearance of design. It is that when there are genetic mutations in a group, and some of those differences provide a survival advantage, then those helpful differences will be passed on down the line. Survival-friendly genes have a "unfair" advantage. The last tenet (evolutionary change by nonselective means) is that some events may help out with evolution without using natural selection, as, for example, when different groups have differing numbers of offspring. This means that some changes "have nothing to do with adaptation" (p. 13).

Okay, so back to Paley. When we find a watch in the woods, we may infer a watchmaker. Not so fast, Coyne says, and then provides us with an alternative way of getting to the watch. Now most creationist critiques at this point show that it is not quite so simple as all that, and argue with the alternative way of getting to the watch. I am entirely on board with all of that, but want to make another point. But before getting to my different point, however, let me just tip my hat to the traditional critiques—which I will no doubt be offering myself later on in this book review. For one example, the chasm between inorganic and organic is enormous, and it is a gap for which Coyne's six component parts of evolution have absolutely no relevance. So what happened *there*? For another example, why should any of the genetic changes confer any survival advantage at all? And so forth.

But here is the different point, one that grants, for the sake of the argument, that Coyne has offered us a way of getting to a watch without a watchmaker. That still doesn't prove that there was no watchmaker . . . but Coyne thinks it does.

Once the mechanism of natural selection was pointed out, Coyne thinks the discussion is over.

"The more one learns about plants and animals, the more one marvels at how well their designs fit their ways of life. What could be more natural than inferring that this fit reflects *conscious* design? Yet Darwin looked beyond the obvious, suggesting—and supporting with copious evidence—two ideas that forever dispelled the idea of deliberate design. Those ideas were evolution and natural selection" (p. 3).

Now look at what he does here. There are two possible explanations for something, one kind of obvious, and the other far-fetched. Darwin, and Coyne after him, show that the far-fetched option is a possibility, yay, and Coyne therefore thinks this "forever dispelled" the other option. But to show that something with the appearance of design *might* have been the result of an impersonal process does not show that it *had* to have been the result of an impersonal process. How could that follow? To go from the possibility of no God to the certainty of no God is an exercise in wish fulfillment.

If Paley's companion, arguing with him, showed (with copious evidence) that the watch could have assembled itself, why can Paley not still reply that he thinks it is simpler to surmise that somebody lost his watch. "Look. There is a name inscribed on the back of it. William of Occam. And here's his shaving kit. It has a razor in it."

This is to argue, in effect, that if there is the slightest possibility that there is no God, then we must conclude decisively that there is no God. But to go from "there might not be a designer" to "there must not be a designer" is a great leap—almost as great as the leap from inorganic to organic, and like that earlier chasm, there is no natural selection to help you get across it.

This is because bad arguments, being inorganic, don't have any genetic material.

CHAPTER 2

That's a Rabbit, You Doofus

Comes now Chapter Two of Coyne's book, called "Written in the Rocks." It will take a post or two to deal with this chapter, so patience, all of you.

My first post will address the structure of his argumentation, and later I will look at the time involved in all this—my own variation on what is called Haldane's Dilemma.

First, we may take as an indicator of how Coyne represents data generally by how he represents the position of his adversaries. He refers to the "creationist prediction that all species must appear suddenly and then remain unchanged" (p. 32). As stated, this is simplistic and wrong, and when he tries to qualify it a moment later, he misrepresents even as he qualifies.

"Even some creationists will admit that minor changes in size and shape might occur over time—a process called *microevolution*—but they reject the idea that one *very different* kind of animal or plant can some from another (*macroevolution*)" (pp. 32-33).

It is not "*some* creationists *admit* that changes *might* happen." It is *all* creationists *insist* changes *have* happened.

Variation within kinds, including significant variation, is not something that any competent creationist denies. Indeed, it is an essential part of the creationist model.

That said, here is the problem with the structure of Coyne's argument. Recall the elementary school exercise where the teacher would give you ten vocabulary words and your job was to write a creative little story using those words. But with such an exercise, it is hard to get things wrong, as long as you complete the assignment. The story is yours to write. But suppose the situation were more like what we have before us in the fossil record. Suppose you had a set number of vocabulary words, and your job was to reconstruct the book they came from—*War and Peace*, say. The fossils we have are the vocabulary words we have to use, and the entire history of all living organisms is the book we must reconstruct. Suppose further that the words we had to work with came down to us entirely and completely by chance, brought to us by wind and tide.

How much do we know? What happens when we hold it up against what we don't know? Coyne acknowledges part of this, and is oblivious to the other. Here they are—one, two.

"We can estimate that we have fossil evidence of only 0.1 percent to 1 percent of all species—hardly a good sample of the history of life" (p. 22).

Well stated, good start, but . . .

"Nevertheless, we have enough fossils to give us a good idea of how evolution proceeded" (p. 22).

The results of the rest of the chapter are akin to what happened with the Piltdown man—building up quite a story about Mr. and Mrs. Piltdown, and all from the tooth of an extinct pig. There is no dispute that Coyne is using all his assigned vocabulary, and he is doing so creatively and with great ingenuity. He is a learned man. But the novel he has reconstructed is not *War and Peace*, but rather *Tom Swift and the Alien Robot*.

It might be complained that my illustration of a novel is unfair because words don't have a lineage from earlier words used in the book, and what we have with evolution is a huge, gigantic family tree. Right—and 99% of the tree is missing, and you are trying to reconstruct it, on the supposition that it is a tree, and you don't even know *that*, and you are doing it with a dogmatic and serene aplomb.

"No theory of special creation or *any* theory other than evolution, can explain these patterns" (p. 29).

Oh. Glad somebody told us. There we were, wasting our time . . . Actually, I would be glad to acknowledge that the creationism he has in his mind is not able to explain these patterns, because the creationism he is fighting with in there is unable by definition to explain anything.

So let me change the illustration. You are doing genealogical research of a family over 100,000 years, and all you have is photographs of .01 percent of the noses, and no ancestry.com, no records, no family Bibles, and so on. You don't even know if it is a family line. Now comparing what you actually know (your nose photographs) with what you acknowledge you do not and cannot know (everything else), could we have a little humility please?

One final comment, not so much an argument.

"Asked what observation could conceivably disprove evolution, the curmudgeonly biologist J. B. S. Haldane reportedly growled, "Fossil rabbits in the Precambrian!" (p. 53).

I just want to state for the record that if I ever found one, I wouldn't bother to take it in, knowing that I could not be believed. "What do you mean Precambrian? That's a *rabbit*, you doofus."

CHAPTER 3
Like Watching a Hummingbird Fly

As previously mentioned, here is my second installment on chapter two of Coyne's book. As this chapter makes apparent, long stretches of time are essential to the project of evolutionary hand-waving, a process whereby impossible things are made more plausible to us by having them happen very, very slowly. Don't think I can walk across that swimming pool? Watch this as I inch my way out there. Bet I can do it if a spend three months at it. Time fixes all implausibilities.

Going with Coyne's figure of 600 million years of evolution in 4th gear, after leaving out those halcyon days of one-celled organisms just bobbing about, not to mention the subsequent time of the eukaryotes (p. 28), and not messing with leap years, we come up with, using a simple arithmetical process, 219,000,000,000 days available for evolution. Roll that around in your mind for a moment. All the marvels that evolution has wrought were accomplished in a matter of countable *days*. This has ramifications.

I said earlier that I was going to be offering a variation on Haldane's Dilemma, but before getting to my version, let my brother Gordon (the scientist) explain Haldane:

> That said, we know the entire genomes of both humans and chimps. There are 40-45 million nucleotide bases present in humans that are missing from chimps, as well as about the same number present in chimps that are absent from humans. This amounts to ~40 million separate mutation events that would need to occur to separate these two kinds. These two creatures are supposedly separated by 300,000 generations. This means that about 133 mutations need to be fixed in a population's genome every generation. This is a huge problem and is called "Haldane's Dilemma" because it is empirically untenable to assume that that staggering number of mutations could be fixed in comparatively few numbers of generations. 'Fixed in a population' means that it can't just happen to one individual. A beneficial mutation needs to spread to most members of the population and that has to happen by passing it down to your descendants with the help of natural selection promoting the mutation's success. This of course requires several generations to let it spread.

In this form, evolutionists think they have enough of an answer to dismiss creationists as chumps for advancing it (and for those interested, you can always pursue it further with a quick web search). In my view, their current responses are just more hand-waving, but allow me to restate the problem in a variant form. Here the problem is more statistical and mathematical, while Haldane's problem was more strictly biological. The common factor in these arguments is the amount of time available for what needed to have happened.

Coyne tells us that the estimated number of species that have lived could be as high as 4 billion (p. 22). Let's take that number to illustrate the point, knowing that the same point can still be made with a different number.

With four billion species out there, let us surmise a crazy low number of genetic changes in one species to turn it into another one—ten changes, let's say. But ten changes per species with four billion species means that we need forty billion beneficial mutations in order to account for all these different species that showed up at one time or another. So let's divide this 40 billion into how many days we are working with. That means that in the history of evolution, a beneficial mutation would need to be happening, on average, somewhere on earth to some critter every 5 or 6 days or so.

But wait. In order to "register" as a beneficial change, making room for the next change to also register, it has to confer a survival advantage—because the central mechanism that makes evolution go is natural selection. But it has to confer this survival advantage in less than a week.

Now I am not assuming that all species are lined up in a series, with a direct line from our most distant ancestor straight down to us. In short, I am not assuming "no cousins." I am not lining all these species up in a straight line, as though there were no cousins or distant cousins. I am just saying that something marvelous has to be happening in evolutionary history constantly, somewhere on the planet. A number of these lines can be running in parallel, but the ones that successfully make it to the next species have to be running in series for their ten changes at some point. The bridge has to make it all the way across the river.

In order to register in the fossil record, in most instances it has to make it all the way across the bridge to the next species, since we have very few transitional forms in hand. But this means that the statistical average time span for the transition from one species to another would be just over a couple of months. It needn't be this quick for all of them, of course. I am just talking about the *averages*.

If evolution happened in a matter of countable days, and if we have had as many species as we have, we can calculate what the average pace of beneficial evolutionary events would have to have been. And remember, if you stretch out the time for one transition to happen with any ancestor, you are shortening the time available for any descendants.

One other thing. The odds of flipping a coin to heads ten times in a row is 1 in 1024. Those are the odds for our ten changes from species to species if each change presented itself as a simple heads/tails possibility. But of course, mutations present many more options than just two. I will leave the rest of that to our statistician friends out there. Suppose at each genetic fork in the road there were just ten options instead of two. The coins have 9 sides other than heads. What would the odds be of flipping the right choice ten times in a row then? And remember, when you have flipped, you don't just look at it and say *heads*. You have to wait 6 days (on average) to see if any survival advantage was conferred.

Now make the final adjustment. Ten changes from species to species is absurdly low. A one in ten chance for the mutation to be beneficial is absurdly low. The chances that we will get identifiable survival advantage in less than a week is absurdly low. Get yourself a real calculator, one that goes up to the decillions, and enter the real numbers. The one thing you will not be able to do after that point is dismiss as an idiot someone who has trouble believing in this high speed miracle of yours with no God around. For mark my words, once the real numbers are entered, observing the process of evolution would be like watching a hummingbird fly.

The trouble for evolutionists is that they set the evolutionary chronology back when we had no idea of the staggering complexities that go into even one-celled organisms. The chronological framework was set for them, and poured into concrete, back when we thought 600 million years was plenty of time. It reminds me of the time when I had a computer that had 10 megabytes of memory, which I thought cavernous. And the more complexity we find, which we are doing all the time, the more we have to fit into our 219,000,000,000 days. That's *days*, people.

It is starting to look as though we won't have to even speed that time lapse camera up, and what I really want to do is go watch it in an IMAX theater.

CHAPTER 4

Evolutionary Heritage Days

The next chapter of Coyne's book is on vestigia, atavistic throwbacks, embryonic recapitulation, topped off with alleged screw-ups in the so-called process of intelligent design.

Let's start with this last item, since we should be able to dispense with it in a paragraph or so. The structure of this argument is strange, in that Coyne is trying to disprove the existence of automotive engineers by showing that carburetors can get gummed up. The reason Coyne falls into this trap is that he is failing to interact with the entire creationist narrative, which is creation *and fall.* The point is not that everything about the world is perfect in every way, but rather that the universe exhibits design everywhere we look, even in those places where some of the features of that design are busted. Their bustedness is *part of the narrative*, so finding examples of it doesn't refute anybody or anything. Paley's argument from the watch could still work even if we found a watch that wasn't ticking. The argument could still work even though the watch wasn't. But Coyne says:

"Perfect design would truly be the sign of a skilled and intelligent designer. *Imperfect* design is the mark of evolution; in fact, it's precisely what we *expect* from evolution" (p. 81).

Imperfect design is also something we would expect to find in a created *and fallen* order.

When it comes to vestigia (like the appendix) or atavisms (like whale legs or human tails), there are two ways to engage with the argument. One is to deny that the data is being represented fully, fairly or accurately, and the other is to grant the data and point out that it doesn't necessarily mean what is being claimed for it. I would want to reject the idea that God put a bunch of false leads into the created order so that He might test our faith (p. 85).

Creationists do not have a problem granting that variations (some of them significant) can occur over time within the classification of "kinds" (Gen. 1:21). Take the lowly skink, for example. Out of all of the skinks, some have legs, some have no legs, and some have various kinds of in-between thingies. If our father Noah took no more than two skinks on board the ark, there is no problem whatever caused for any thinking creationist by the appearance or disappearance of legs in any of the descendants.

One example of atavism that Coyne cites is that of the whale leg. "About one whale in five hundred is actually born with a rear leg that protrudes outside the body wall" (p. 64). My first method of doubt mentioned above would want to ask questions—how far outside the body wall does it protrude? Five centimeters? On a whale? Should we call it the leg pimple? Why just one leg? Did they hop? Those bits of bone you found inside it, what are the grounds for identifying one bit (just centimeters long) as a whale tibia, other than that it fits with the "just so" story you are telling?

Reasonable questions, but let's move on to the second approach to evolutionary skepticism. Remember the skink. Some whales do have a pelvis (which has a function for them), but not the function that our pelvis does. Suppose that whales are not descended from really big cows of some sort, as the evolutionary theory demands. Suppose they are descended from other whales, identifiable as such, that used to have flippers in the rear? Suppose whales got tired of being taken for sea lions? or walruses? and so they pulled a skink? If you ask me to prove my hypothesis, I will point proudly to this five centimeter flipper bump. See it flapping?

Embryonic recapitulation is a weird one, because it seems like a odd dependence on something that doesn't really prove anything. The slashes on the side of a human embryo look like the slashes that turn into gills on a fish, but on us they turn into our head and upper body instead. Even on evolutionary assumptions, what would be the point (as in, survival advantage) of having each embryo of every living species go through a historical reenactment of the history of all life heretofore? Is it like having kindergarten kids dress up like Pilgrims at Thanksgiving? Is our time in the womb some kind of evolutionary Heritage Days?

My last comments will be addressed to vestigia, things that are still hanging around but which we have not discovered a function for yet. You can have your appendix taken out, and appear to be no worse for it, which we could not say about the stomach or the pancreas. So why wouldn't we assume that the appendix is a left over from days gone by? Here are a couple of brief responses. First, it *could* be vestigial. Remember that the creation is fallen. Maybe the appendix was something we needed when we were still eating from the tree of life. Second, remember that medical science is still in its infancy. Most of what is going on in the body is still opaque to us, and so I would be leery of pronouncing on anything like this. The fact you can take an appendix out and not have the patient keel over dead is certainly suggestive of something. But perhaps we don't know the whole story yet.

But the place where modern scientific hubris really kicks in is with the whole subject of "junk DNA." and "dead genes" (pp. 66-73). How long have we even known about DNA? Since April of 1953, which means that our knowledge of the existence of DNA is two months older than I am. For pity's sake! It is as though a couple archeologists discovered that the library of Alexandria didn't really burn down, because they found the whole thing buried under sand, got into the first chamber, read two books, and declared the rest of the library worthless. They knew it was worthless because there were countless languages in there that they didn't understand. Just a bunch of gibberish. For an example of some of the pronouncements that ought not to have been made about this, you can check out the book trailer for *The Myth of Junk DNA*.[3]

---

3. Jonathan Wells, "The Myth of Junk DNA," http://www.mythofjunkdna. com (accessed October 23, 2013).

One of the things my friend Mitch Stokes likes to emphasize is the importance of true skepticism.[4] Reading a chapter like this just underscores that point.

---

4. Mitch Stokes, *A Shot of Faith (to the Head): Be a Confident Believer in an Age of Cranky Atheists* (Nashville: Thomas Nelson, 2012).

CHAPTER 5

His Brother Was Joktan, If That Helps

I n his next chapter, Coyne addresses the subject of bio-geography, "the study of the distribution of species on earth" (p. 88). In responding to this chapter, I want to begin by pointing out how much of it was beside the point. Coyne spent a great deal of time and energy showing the various ways that creationists would be wrong if we were maintaining something that was wrong, but which we don't actually hold anyway. Well, *that* was close.

Coyne points to a number of similarities and dis-similarities of critters in various geographical locations, and wonders aloud why God would have gone all over the planet, creating different kinds of animals in such a way as to make us all think they must have evolved.

But of course, Genesis describes the creation of life in one place, that then needed to spread out and "fill" and "multiply," just like the human race needed to.

"And God blessed them, saying, Be fruitful, and multiply, and fill the waters in the seas, and let fowl multiply in the earth. And the evening and the morning were the fifth day"(Gen. 1:22-23).

And whether or not that was the case with the creation account, it was certainly the case when the animals that survived the Flood spread out from *that* one place (Gen. 8:19). So Coyne's argument engageth with the air, failing to connect.

Coyne accounts for these variations and such by postulating that there was originally one monster continent that has since divided up into the continents we know and love today. But this is beside the point as well. There would be obvious differences about time frames and so forth, but creationists are at least open to the possibility that the continents were once attached to each other. (I will say in passing that if Coyne wants to engage with biblical creationists, as distinct from our ID friends, he needs to have a better grasp of what is involved in Flood geology. He is not engaging with the arguments otherwise.)

For example, Genesis has a cryptic reference to something big that happened a few generations after the Flood. Shem's great-great-grandson was named Peleg, and in his days "the earth was divided" (Gen. 10:21-25). We are not quite sure what this means, but his brother was Joktan, if that helps any. Some creationists believe this represents a continental rupture (as distinct from the continents drifting inches a year for millions of years). As soon as you allow that as a possibility, Coyne's argument curls up in a ball and won't stop whimpering.

But I must also say that even though creationists are not necessarily opposed to the idea of one super-continent existing at one time, everyone who loves God rightly must unite to oppose Coyne's name for that continent, which is Gondwana. I am sure he got this name from what he thought was a reputable source, but in this he was tragically mistaken. Gondwana sounds like a backward province of a country that ought not to be allowed to sit on the United Nations Human Rights Council. It sounds like it was named by a couple of paleo-geologists who were up too late at one of their conferences, having had one too many beers, and who then started naming things in a cluster of giggles.

Now when you combine this with what I previously pointed out about the creationist acknowledgment of significant variation within kinds, Coyne's efforts in this chapter really are beside the point. But still, even with that noted, it should also be mentioned that Coyne believes that the only kind of god who is allowed into his thought experiments is a god who has the mentality of some dullard bureaucrat, the kind who sleeps at his desk so often that one side of his head is flat, and who consequently has no imagination at all.

"Why would a creator put plants that are fundamentally different, but look so similar in diverse areas of the world that seem ecologically identical? Wouldn't it make more sense . . ." (p. 91).

"If animals were specially created, why would the creator produce on different continents fundamentally different animals that nevertheless look and act so much alike?" (p. 92)

"All they can do is invoke the inscrutable whims of the creator" (p. 92).

Given what creationists actually argue for, Coyne is just shooting his revolvers into the air. But suppose we did think what Coyne alleges. Suppose God did not fill up the world by having all living creatures fan out from one place like it was the Oklahoma land rush. Suppose we thought what Coyne thinks we think. Why then ask questions like "why would God . . ."? The God who created the giraffe, the peacock, the walrus, and the toucan, for just a rudimentary indication, cannot be relied upon to take this question as seriously as Coyne would like Him to. God keeps messing around. *And now, we really need a mammal that lays eggs . . . and what other parts do we have left? . . . a duck bill!* Just *the thing.*

Now all this is just bundles of fun to address, but I do want to make one other point, one that I am not sure Coyne really meant to introduce. This chapter is all about biogeography, and he presents, as one of the central jewels in his argument, the fact that Darwin predicted that fossils of the first paleo-humans would be found in . . . Africa. And then, son of gun, they were (pp. 96-97). But what on earth would possess Darwin to make such a prediction? Well, there would be distribution of species n' stuff, and biogeography . . . and scientific racism.

Coyne quoted Haeckel earlier in this book, which is not necessarily a sin, but he was not quoting him in order to hoot and throw popcorn. Coyne failed to note that, when quoting Haeckel on the embryo argument, he was quoting a man who also believed that "*the differences between the highest and the lowest human is greater than that between the lowest human and the highest animal*" (Ernst Haeckel, *Generelle Morphologie*, II/435, emphasis original). Later, Haeckel divided the human race into 10-12 *species*, and grouped them together in four *genera*. Lest anyone mistake his meaning, he published a chart of twelve profiles, the top six being human, and the bottom six being our simian cousins. Number 1 was a European (Yay, Europe! Yay, science!). Number 5 was a black African, and number 6 was a Tasmanian. Then, just *inches* of stellar scientific reasoning below *that*, came the gorilla. Is everybody still proud of the fact that Darwin called our point of origin for Africa beforehand?

Now this scientific racism (in which Darwin fully participated) got all tied up with the eugenics craze, as well as tied up with the increasingly accepted theory of evolution, and lots of scientific, chin-stroking words like biogeography. In the Introduction to *The Descent of Man*, Darwin said that one of the three goals of his book was to show "the value of the differences between the so-called races of man." He *needed* that as part of his argument.

This was before eugenics and the rest of all this foolishness covered itself with dishonor in the heyday of scientific racism, the German version, and so it was still possible back then for scientists to talk about differences in humans the way Coyne talks about finches. Since they could, they did. Since Coyne can't, he doesn't, but I would love to be present at a Q & A session where for some reason they couldn't turn my microphone off. I will put it this way—on the principles Coyne has been arguing for here, the theory of evolution justifies scientific racism as a clear possibility. It must be on the table. If we all evolved from a common ancestor, and if there are diverse populations of us, and if the rate of evolution is not a fixed constant like 9.8 meters per second squared, it follows that somebody could easily be a lot closer to that common ancestor than somebody else. Follow the argument wherever it leads, man. I thought scientists were supposed to be courageous.

But—in stark contrast to this folly—biblical Christians have always believed the entire human race consists of *cousins*. We are all one in Adam, we are one in Noah, and we are offered in the gospel the opportunity of being all one in Christ. Moreover, the racial differences between humans demonstrate how much monogenistic Christians believe that significant variation *within a single kind* can easily occur. And what this also means, taking it one step further, is that Coyne knows what *he* believes, but he has only the faintest grasp of what the people he is seeking to refute believe. Not a good showing.

CHAPTER 6
Evolution's Alligatornado

C oyne's next chapter is on the "engine of evolution," which is to say, natural selection. One of his examples was one I was already familiar with, and since it is quite a fun one—let's just go with it.

There is a kind of roundworm that is a parasite to a species of ant in Central America. I will just give you the short form here. An infected ant has its normally black abdomen turn a bright red. The ant is made sluggish by the parasite, and his now red abdomen is made to stick straight up into the air, looking for all the world like an edible berry, at least to birds. In addition, the connection between the thorax and the abdomen is weakened, making it easier for a bird to pick that berry (p. 113). And while ants normally can produce a pheromone which warn the other ants of an attack, the pheromones in the infected ant are all shut down. Got all that?

A bird comes down and scarfs the berry, which is full of roundworm eggs. Those eggs are passed on through in the bird droppings, which other ants think would be good to scavenge in order to get food for their larvae back home. Taken back to the ant colony, these roundworm eggs hatch inside the pupae, and the worms head on down to the abdomen to mate and produce more eggs, and make the abdomen red and berry-like.

Now anyone who can read an account like this, while stipulating that it must be the result of natural processes flying blind, without laughing out loud, is simply not paying attention.

"It is staggering adaptations like this—the many ways that parasites control their carriers, just to pass on the parasites' genes—that gets an evolutionist's juices flowing" (p. 113).

That word *staggering* is right, and what we know about such processes is scarcely a fraction of what is actually going on. And it is going on everywhere.

To his credit, Coyne admits how it *looks*. "Everywhere we look in nature, we see animals that *seem* beautifully designed to fit their environment" (p. 115). At the same time, he denies that natural selection is blind. He acknowledges that the chance mutations are blind, but argues that the filtering of such mutations by natural selection is manifestly *not* random (p. 119). The cards are shuffled by chance, but the invisible poker playing hand (natural selection) renders everything reasonable and scientific. The only problem is that the hand is not attached to a head, but is pretty smart anyway.

So this means my first point in response to all this is something that Coyne would cheerfully grant, and indeed says himself. But I want to say it stronger. All this means that the roundworm in our example does not know *anything*. It does not know that there is such a thing as an ant, or an abdomen, or a thorax, or a berry, or a bird, or bird droppings, or a roundworm. It is not *doing* anything. It is just propagating along, and then a mutation happens. Coyne acknowledges that "most [mutations] are harmful or neutral" (p. 118). He goes on to say that a "few can turn out to be useful." "The useful ones are the raw material for evolution" (p. 118).

The engine of evolution breaks down a lot, but it still drives everything everywhere.

And this is where I need to jump ahead to another part of the chapter where Coyne interacts (very inadequately) with the ID argument of "irreducible complexity," articulated most effectively in Michael Behe's *Darwin's Black Box.* Coyne's one-sentence statement of irreducible complexity is accurate as far as it goes, which is not very far, but which after that gets really lame pretty rapidly. The first sentence below is his summary.

"IDers argue that such traits, involving many parts that must cooperate for that trait to function at all defy Darwinian explanation. Therefore, by default, they must have been designed by a supernatural agent. This is commonly called the 'God of the gaps' argument, and it is an argument from ignorance" (p. 137).

Since the citation above concludes with the word *ignorance*, now would be a good time to point how that Coyne doesn't have the faintest idea of how his opponent's arguments actually work. For a scholar to argue this way, with the banner of knowledge snapping smartly above his head, is simply disgraceful. Better an argument *from* ignorance than an argument *in* ignorance, that's the first thing. And second, Behe's argument isn't an argument from ignorance. It is an argument from our *knowledge* of complex systems.

Irreducible complexity is an argument which engages with the claims for natural selection, and does so at every step of the process. Take Behe's simple illustration of a mousetrap. In order to build an evolutionary mousetrap, it is not sufficient to give yourself hundreds of thousands of years in which to wait patiently for the mousetrap to evolve and to then confer a staggering survival advantage all at once. The argument requires that each step of the process confer a significant survival advantage, all by itself. Coyne acknowledges the necessity of this, but then proceeds blithely on his way with his nose in the air.

This is a serious argument, one which (in the details) Coyne just ignores. He is either ignoring it because he is ignorant in the old-fashioned way, or he is ignoring it because he knows that he has no answer to the argument, and decided to blow smoke instead.

To take Behe's mousetrap example, you can't have a mutation that gives you a small wooden platform, which catches the occasional mouse, thus conferring a slight survival advantage. The wood platform wouldn't catch anything, and would just get the way. And no bird would mistake it for a berry.

Then *the next thing you can't have* is a hundred thousand years of dragging around a small wooden platform, as you wait for the mutation that produces a spring that rests uselessly on that platform, doing nothing also, just like the platform, but somehow resulting in a few more mice being caught. No, the whole mousetrap must be there, completely assembled, in order to do anything helpful at all. It is an irreducibly complex system.

Back to the roundworm. He doesn't know anything about this argument, so his mutations keep turning the ant abdomen into replicas of berries that birds detest, into camo-skin that hides the ants better than they were hidden before, and into little pebble replicas. When he finally hits on the red berry, yay, it was at the same time that another uncooperative mutation made the attack pheromone release in triple amounts, so that the other ants were in a state of constant vigilance. Not only that, but another mutation made the attachment of abdomen and thorax a super-strong one, and also made the ant particularly energetic, not sluggish, and yet another mutation made the red abdomen droop down between the ant legs where the birds couldn't see it. So then we had to wait for another one hundred thousand trips around the sun for the red berry thing to happen again, but this time with the pheromones shut off, and the abdomen attachment weakened, and the ants interested in hunting down roundworm eggs, which they came to believe were just the thing for their larvae.

Not only that, but we have to explain what's in it for the ants. We can see at once that this exquisite system confers survival advantages on the roundworm. But why aren't the ants mutating themselves a red berry hider? All you need is a hundred thousand years, and some ants still alive at the end of it.

So then, in building this system, you are not just rolling one dice with fifty sides. You are rolling ten die at the same time, each one with fifty sides. And you are doing this, or something equivalent, on every third leaf in the jungle. Evolution advances, inexorably, on the strength of a Powerball winner every ten minutes.

Whenever you are telling a fictional story, the one thing you must not lose is "the willing suspension of disbelief" on the part of the audience. One writing coach (a gent named Bickham) advises fiction writers to avoid dropping "an alligator through the transom." You lose people when they say, "Oh, for pity's sake!"

In the early years of evolutionary theory, there was an awful lot we didn't know about the staggering complexity of life forms, all the way up to the elephants and whales, and all the way down to flagellated bacteria. But now our scientific knowledge is advancing so rapidly that evolutionists, in order to keep telling us their "just so" story, have to drop an alligator through the transom on a more or less continual basis. It is raining alligators. Better yet, we have gotten to that tipping point of scientific knowledge has finally gotten its big break, and has been allowed to write the screenplay for *Alligatornado*.

This chapter also has a section where Coyne argues from the success of animal breeders.

"If *artificial* selection can produce such canine diversity so quickly, it becomes easier to accept that the lesser diversity of wild dogs arose by *natural* selection acting over a period of a thousand times longer" (p. 126).

I see. The fact that a farmer in Nebraska can grow a thousand acres of corn, all of it in straight rows, makes it easier to believe that this could eventually happen by itself, if only we give it enough time? The fact that something can happen when tended is an argument for not having to tend things?

So one last thing, and I will leave this chapter be. If the Creator packaged the capacity for striking diversity within kinds (as He plainly did with the dog), how is the existence of a striking diversity an argument against God having done that?

CHAPTER 3

The Turtle on the Fencepost

As providence would have it, last night I read the next chapter of Coyne's book in order to mull over it a bit before writing my next post. And then this morning, as is my practice, I spend some time reading through any magazines that have accumulated during the course of the week. And, as I mentioned, as providence would have it, part of that stack was the very fine magazine *Salvo*, which I am happy to commend to you.

Coyne's sixth chapter was "How Sex Drives Evolution." The cover article for this issue of *Salvo* was a great article by Richard Stevens on how sex and mating rituals exhibit (and require) intelligent design.[5]

First, Coyne's chapter was embarrassing in its own right. He points out the staggering complexity involved in the matter of sex, and then gives an evolutionary account of various trifles. He explains things that don't require much explanation (such as how the non-survival

---

5. Richard W. Stevens, "Software for Sex: Successful Mating Habits Require Intelligent Programming," *Salvo* 25 (Summer 2013), http://www.salvomag.com/new/articles/salvo25/software-for-sex.php (accessed October 23, 2013).

of a male is still consistent with the survival of a bunch of his offspring), and leaves untouched the screamers that demand an accounting for anybody who has thought about the problem for more than five minutes.

He does allude to one of those screamers in passing. "Why sex evolved is in fact one of evolution's greatest mysteries" (p. 155). True enough, and no kidding. But then he goes on to explain something else entirely—he solemnly explains how species that already reproduce sexually might avoid mutating back to a system of asexual reproduction.

It is as though he said, "How the turtle got on top of the fence post is one of the greatest mysteries we have. Perhaps I can help by explaining how he might get down off of it."

And this is a good place to bring Stevens' insights into the discussion. One of the things that materialistic evolutionists cannot get their minds around is the fact that information—programming, software, code—does not weigh anything and is not any particular color. Information is *not material*. There is a difference between arguing that an artifact displays the marks of intelligence having been there (as a broken watch still might) and arguing that another artifact requires an intelligent programmer to crank out the code that the system needs to runs on. Both kinds of intelligence need to be explained away by the evolutionist—but they somehow think they only need to explain the first kind, and they don't do *that* very well.

The fact that the symbol *m* represents an *em* sound is not something that is physically resident in that letter. It is part of a code, and codes were coded by somebody. The assumption that evolutionists make, as Stevens points out, is that if a creature has legs, it can just walk. If it has wings, it can just fly. If it has sexual organs, it can just mate.

No. That is like saying that if you have the computer hardware you can do without the software. Believing in the "evolution" of the hardware is a stretch already, but then there is the programming involved. Sexual behaviors are enormously complicated information systems. And, as Stevens shows, the information is needed *prior to the behavior itself.*

There are a host of things that creatures can do in their behavior, provided they have a pre-programmed control system that will enable them to do that particular thing. In order to mate—as the examples Coyne uses plainly show, but which he does not see—there must be a cascading system of *if, then* choices, made by both the male and the female. In addition, there is the complexity involved in pattern recognition, both sending and receiving—chirping of the cricket, the croaking of frogs, the bling collection of the bowerbirds, and so forth. This is not something that these creatures "just do" because they have the equipment for doing it. Their behavior is driven by something. Their behavior exhibits intelligence, and *not theirs.* It exhibits the intelligence of the one who wrote the code.

In other words, according to evolution, the hardware has to evolve by chance, and the programming has to evolve simultaneously, also by chance, and the programming can't be iOS trying to run on a Windows PC. Not only that, but the reciprocal elements (to whatever it is that just happened by chance) have to simultaneously happen over in the other sex, hardware and software both, and all of it has to happen at the same time, and within walking, swimming, or flying distance. And this has to happen thousands and thousand of times, over and over again.

And I am not even counting non-behavioral mating aspects, like the eyespots on a peacock's tail. I mean, he doesn't even know that they are back there.

And then, on top of everything else, Coyne fails to show how abandoning asexual reproduction in the first place could possibly confer any kind of survival advantage. When you can already reproduce all by yourself, how are you doing anything to advance the cause by taking half your genetic material necessary for survival, and sending it off somewhere else? Now he might never call. What kind of sense did that move make?

CHAPTER 8
If Creationists Were Beetles

So then, Jerry Coyne now comes to explain, in the famous phrase, the origin of species. How is it that wherever we look we see distinct species, and not a long blur of intermediate types and missing links between each of the species?

In addressing this question, he sets out laboriously to prove something that nobody denies, which is that there are distinct types of animals, that there are variations within kinds, and that there are often wide spaces between them. He notes that the natives of the Arfak Mountains in New Guinea recognized 136 different types of local birds, while Western zoologists had come up with 137 species. This "should convince us, that the discontinuities of nature are not arbitrary, but an objective fact" (p. 169). Well, okay, but was anyone arguing the point?

Coyne argues that such species usually arise because of some kind of geographical separation—mountain ranges, islands, two sides of a river—which allows for certain traits to be reinforced and for others to fade into the background. Later in the chapter, he also notes how certain distinct species can arise through a fun and interesting process called *polyploidy*, where the chromosomes of a particular species are doubled.

But for the most part, he is simply pointing to how physical factors can cause certain populations to be isolated from others, and there, mingling among themselves, to do naturally what dog breeders have been doing for a long time. Speaking of species, in this Coyne is arguing against a species of creationism that doesn't exist. The most ardent fundamentalist creationist acknowledges cheerfully that all the races of men descended from Noah and Mrs. Noah, and that there is (self-evidently) variation within kinds.

So allow me to say this again. Coyne clearly does not know who he is talking *to*, and consequently does not know what he is talking *about*.

"It also counts as evidence against creationism. After all, there's no obvious reason why a creator would produce similar species of birds, or lizards on continents but not on isolated islands. (By 'similar,' I mean so similar that evolutionists would regard them as close relatives. Most creationists do not accept species as 'relatives' since that presupposes evolution)" (p. 185).

On the contrary, if we are talking about evolutionary taxonomy—what evolutionists call "species"—*all* creationists acknowledge that numerous species are related to each other.

Our dispute is not over whether bigger beaks can come from smaller beaks, or furrier beasts from less furry beasts, or shorter tails from longer tails, or light skin from darker skin. In 1937, evolutionist Theodosius Dobzhansky coined the terms microevolution and macroevolution in order to reluctantly note that we had to try to account for macro changes (which we couldn't see happening) on the basis of micro changes (which we could). Some evolutionists, like Dobzhansky, see the problem; some, like Coyne, are blissfully unaware; and others, like me and my fellow non-evolutionists, believe that what is called macroevolution cannot successfully be accounted for by piling up microevolutionary changes.

So the creationist is *not* someone who denies what is called microevolution. The creationist is one who denies that microevolution is a set of "baby steps" sufficient to account for the transformation to another kind of animal entirely. If such a transformation were simply a long, arduous trek, then baby steps will get you there eventually. But is the transformation from no skeleton to an exoskeleton, or no skeleton to endoskeleton, the equivalent of a long walk, where each step is just like the previous one, or is it more like a "back to the drawing board" kind of thing?

I am not a scientist, as Coyne is, but I am a polemicist, and since Coyne decided to engage in some polemical science, he has to that extent come onto my turf. And I can say that, as a simple matter of craft competence, he is in way over his head, and needs to go back to counting his *Drosophilia. He does not understand the tenets of the position he is seeking to refute.* If creationists were a kind of beetle, Coyne ought not to write a book calling us spiders.

I should note on other thing. Coyne makes a nice little blunder when he tries to wave his hands over a problem caused by the passing of the years.

"How fast would speciation need to be able to explain the present diversity of life? It's been estimated that there are 10 million species on earth today. Let's raise that to 100 million to take into account undiscovered species. It turns out that if you started with a single species 3.5 billion years ago, you could get 100 million species living today even if each ancestral species split into two descendants only once every 200 million years. As we've seen, real speciation happens a lot faster than that . . ." (p. 179).

Remind me sometime to tell you the story of the man who drowned in a river that was on average only six inches deep. How could such a thing have possibly happened? Let us clear our throats and look at these numbers a little quizzically. Coyne has earlier said that the number of species on earth could have been as high as 4 billion (p. 22), not 100 million (p. 179), and he has earlier acknowledged that the vast majority of the speciation occurred in the last 600 million years (p. 28), not in the last 3.5 billion (p. 179). In other words, between pages 22-28 and page 179, there is a whole lot of fudging going on, which is to say, we are not trying to get 100 million species into 3.5 billion years. It is more like we are trying to get 4 billion species into 600 million years, which is quite a different problem of division. Wouldn't you say?

CHAPTER 9

Kicking Evolutionary Euro-Butt

oyne's last two chapters might best be treated together. This is because the closer we get to the end, the faster the evolution of this review wants to accelerate.

In these chapters, Coyne addresses the evolution of man. Chapter 8, "What About Us?," tackles the evolution of man, and his last chapter, "Evolution Redux," also about us, tries to whistle up meaning from the void.

To his credit, Coyne at least tries to tackle the thorny topic of race as it relates to evolution.

"In *The Descent of Man*, Darwin had conjectured that our species had originated in Africa because our closest relatives, gorillas and chimpanzees, are both found there" (p. 191).

Darwin also thought this because early evolutionists believed that blacks, also found there, were the closest human relatives of those primates. Coyne keeps Darwin and other worthies out of it, but he does acknowledge the problem. "From the beginning of modern biology, racial classification has gone hand in hand with racial prejudice" (p. 212).

What he doesn't adequately reckon with is the fact that such "prejudice" ought not, on evolution's terms, be kept off the table. There have been creationists who have been racially bigoted, but when they were, it was contrary to their foundational beliefs about a common descent from Adam and from Noah. But if evolutionists came across a lost valley somewhere that had a tribe of "people" that walked upright, had a language with 500 words in it, and were four feet tall, what would they do with them? If we are related to the primates, is it automatically prejudice to try to figure out if some of us are *closer* relations than others?

Without entering the debates himself, Coyne reveals how particular the debates about human speciation can get.

"Whether a humanlike fossil is named as one species or another can turn on matters as small as half a millimeter in the diameter of a tooth, or slight differences in the shape of a thighbone" (p. 197).

As though differences between individuals didn't display much greater variations than that! Their fossil history of the human race is like the vocabulary exercise I mentioned before, where a child is given ten words and told to work them into a story. The fact that all the words can be made to fit does not mean the story actually happened. And we are not talking a short little elementary school story. We are talking about ten thousand Russian novels, and we still have just ten vocabulary words. We are talking about millions of years and a relative handful of bones.

There are three basic considerations that need to be taken into account, which Coyne does not do. The first is that evolution doesn't have a notion of progress built into the science of it. Evolution is all about surviving, and not about listening to the symphony. That means that "up" is a metaphor, and it is not necessary for the "advanced" species to be the descendant. If we all devolve to cockroaches, that would be fine, provided there are a bunch of us carrying our genes into the glory of that wonderful future.

Second, Coyne has consistently refused to acknowledge that creationists believe in variation within kinds, and they believe in variations significant enough that were a evolutionary paleontologist to find a couple sets of bones from two variants, he would call them distinct species. Creationists believe that Goliath was a blood cousin to the pygmies.

And third, related to the second, it would be the work of a ten minute thought experiment to take an animal kind—the dog, let us say—pretend we had never seen one, and then to dig up the bones of a little lap dog, a spaniel, a Rottweiler, and an Irish wolfhound, and then construct a story about how the big ones came from the little ones. We could get from a circus pony to a Percheron the same way. But weaving the story doesn't make the threads come into existence.

As he rounds into the straight, Coyne wants to gallop to a glorious finish. Evolution is a "scientific fact" (p. 222). "All the evidence" shows "without a scintilla of doubt" that "organisms have evolved" (p. 222). Evolution "always comes up right" (p. 223). "No serious biologist doubts these propositions" (p. 223).

Fortunately, it is very easy to tell who the serious biologists are, because they are the ones who never doubt these propositions. It is like survival of the fittest, only for biologists. The fittest survive, and we know who the fittest are because they survived. Isn't science wonderful?

Controversies within the evolutionary community are a sign of a "vibrant, thriving field" (p. 223). Disagreements among creationists, on the other hand, indicate a group of cornpones in disarray (p. 208). This is simply a variation on the previous point.

I said earlier that Coyne wanted to whistle up meaning from the void. God has placed eternity in our hearts (Eccl. 3:11), and that cannot be adequately replaced by eons of evolution, however many adjectives you use. "We make symphonies, poems, and books to fulfill our aesthetic passions and emotional needs" (p. 233). We also build churches, and evolutionists want to deconstruct and explain away *that* need. When they are done, the symphonies and poems will be next. Any left over emotional needs can be fixed with sex, *soma*, and the feelies.

But if you lose meaning, and you have a desperate need for it, the only alternative is to make your own out of the surrounding meaninglessness. This has happened within living memory, a fact of history concerning which Coyne appears to be serenely unaware.

"The biggest of these misconceptions is that accepting evolution will somehow sunder our society, wreck our morality, impel us to behave like beasts, and spawn a new generation of Hitlers and Stalins. That just won't happen, as we know from the many European countries whose residents wholly embrace evolution yet manage to remain civilized" (p. 233).

Excuse me for a minute while I make merry with some questions. What was it that produced the *last* generation of Hitlers and Stalins? How long ago was that? Did my father-in-law fight in that war? Did my father join the Navy to fight in that war? Did *I* serve in the Navy to help take down the evil empire that Stalin had consolidated? Why does it seem not all that long ago? And may I be pardoned for wondering what *continent* those bad guys were on? Did they remain civilized throughout the course of that conflict? Or did civilization vanish sometime (when? how? in the grip of what kinds of scientific theories?) and then reboot in 1945? And what was it that happened in 1945? Well, I will tell you. The American creationists (p. 192) kicked some evolutionary butt.

Lightning Source UK Ltd.
Milton Keynes UK
UKHW022359270821
389594UK00013B/2698